Please renew or return items by the date
shown on your receipt

www.hertfordshire.gov.uk/libraries

Renewals and enquiries: 0300 123 4049

Textphone for hearing or 0300 123 4041
speech impaired users:

L32 11.16

526 267 07 X

HOW TO

SET A TABLE

—

EBURY PRESS

CONTENTS

"One cannot think well, love well, sleep well, if one has not dined well."

———

VIRGINIA WOOLF

INTRODUCTION

Whether you're giving a dinner party for twelve or sharing a takeaway for two, a thoughtful setting can make any meal feel special. Formal or casual, traditional or modern, colourful or neutral, patterned or plain, your table should reflect your style.

Trying to keep track of all the rules can seem intimidating. But with a few simple guidelines, almost anything goes. You can mix and match, repurpose pieces, and incorporate vintage finds. Think about dressing a table as if you were putting together a great outfit – personality is always the most important ingredient.

This handbook will help you navigate the nuances of table settings, fill your cupboards with pieces you love, and find new ways to use them in any space. As your tastes evolve, so will your collection. Why not have fun with it?

PICKING YOUR PIECES

Dinnerware Basics

Whichever dishes you decide on, dinnerware is meant to be used. Think about what kinds of food you like to eat and how you tend to entertain, then pick the pieces that make sense. A good number to start with is eight settings, or twelve if you invite guests round regularly.

CHOOSE YOUR TYPE

PORCELAIN

A slightly translucent ceramic made by firing high-quality clays at extremely high temperatures, porcelain is generally very durable, resistant to stains, and dishwasher-, oven-, and microwave-safe (with the exception of metallic or highly decorated pieces) despite its delicate appearance.

EARTHENWARE

Made from less refined clays and fired at lower temperatures, earthenware is porous and less resistant to chipping. Glazes are often added to make pieces more durable and non-absorbent.

STONEWARE

Combining porcelain's resilience with the casual look of earthenware, these chip-resistant and non-porous pieces are made by firing dense clay at high temperatures.

Table **TALK**

BECAUSE THE CHINESE FIRST CAME UP WITH THE FORMULA TO MAKE PORCELAIN, 'CHINA' IS OFTEN USED AS A GENERAL TERM FOR FINE PORCELAIN.

SELECT YOUR SET

Many companies offer dinnerware in four- or five-piece sets. The most common include a dinner plate, a tea or luncheon plate, a bowl, and a mug. A slightly more formal option offers a bread-and-butter plate rather than the bowl, and a cup and saucer instead of the mug.

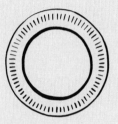

DINNER PLATE

At 25–28 centimetres in diameter, the most common styles are the coupe and traditional rim.

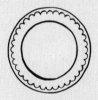

TEA OR LUNCHEON PLATE

From 19–22 centimetres in diameter, this is easily adaptable for salads, desserts, lunch, or afternoon tea.

BOWLS

Rim or coupe, shallow or deep, bowls are traditionally used for soup, pasta, or cereal. Fruit bowls are slightly smaller and are perfect for puddings and vegetable side dishes.

CUPS & SAUCERS

A standard coffee cup holds 180–240 millilitres. A large breakfast cup or mug holds 325–350 millilitres.

ADD À LA CARTE

It's also common to purchase open stock pieces. You can pick each dish individually or add to existing sets. Below are some additional styles to consider:

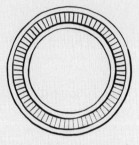

CHARGER

Generally 28–35 centimetres in diameter, this large plate isn't meant to hold food. It serves as a placeholder for the dinner plate and can be left on the table as a base for the tea or luncheon plate, or a soup bowl.

BREAD & BUTTER PLATE

Between 15–16 centimetres, it's also perfectly sized for breakfast or to support stemmed glasses used for serving desserts.

SMALL TEA OR LUNCHEON PLATE

Slightly smaller than a regular tea or luncheon plate, the two can be used interchangeably.

A flexible and economical approach is to pick just a dinner plate and a shallow bowl, which can be used for soup, salad, cereal, and desserts.

CHOOSE YOUR SERVING PIECES

As long as you have a mix of shapes and sizes, these pieces can serve multiple purposes, and they're fun to collect over time.

SOUP TUREEN
Highly decorative yet functional, this is one of the largest serving pieces and includes a cover to keep food warm.

SAUCE BOAT
For gravy as well as sauce, this can be used in combination with a ladle to help avoid spills.

PLATTERS
Whether oval or round, covered or open, these are good for vegetables, grains, and meats.

BOWLS
Large, deep bowls are perfect for salads and side dishes.

If space is an issue, nesting bowls that stack inside one another are a clever choice.

Glasses at a Glance

Designed with specific drinks in mind, certain shapes can enhance flavours and ingredients, but feel free to mix them up.

TUMBLER
Usually made with a 230-millilitre capacity, it's used for water, juice, or soft drinks.

WINE GLASSES
Red wine is best served in larger styles with wide bowls to encourage oxidation. White is served in glasses that are narrower at the top.

CHAMPAGNE GLASSES
A tall, narrow flute helps stop fizz going flat. A shallow, saucer-shaped coupe strikes a vintage vibe.

HIGHBALL
This taller glass is used mainly for mixed drinks, such as gin and tonic.

WHISKY GLASS
Also called a rocks tumbler, this heavy-bottomed glass is used for serving whisky with or without ice and water.

PILSNER OR LAGER GLASS
Tall with a slight taper, it's made to showcase lighter pale ales but can be used for any beer.

BALLOON GLASS
Great for after-dinner drinks, such as armagnac, cognac, or brandy, the balloon-shaped bowl that is narrower at the top helps capture aromas.

Cutlery Essentials

While dozens of speciality pieces were once common, like the asparagus fork and the fruit spoon, today a standard set generally includes five pieces – a dinner knife, two forks (one for dinner, the other for salad or dessert), and two spoons (one larger, which is often also used for soup, the other smaller for tea or coffee).

As with dinnerware, eight to twelve sets is a good place to start. Sterling silver can be expensive but it will last forever. Whichever material or style you choose, look for pieces that have a little bit of weight and a nice feel in the hand.

STERLING SILVER

Recognised by its stamp, sterling silver is mixed with a small amount of hard alloy metal for strength at a ratio of 92.5 per cent pure silver to 7.5 per cent copper.

SILVER PLATE

Less expensive but with the same warmth as sterling, these pieces are made from a base metal such as nickel or copper that is plated with silver.

STAINLESS STEEL

Low maintenance and usually the most common choice, stainless is made from an alloy of iron, chromium, and nickel.

Always shine silver with good-quality polish, rinse well, and dry thoroughly with a soft linen cloth to avoid spotting. Be careful not to polish roughly or too often as too much buffing can take off the top layer, including any monograms.

Salad
FORK

Dinner
FORK

Dinner
KNIFE

Dessert
SPOON

Tea
SPOON

The Linen Drawer

One of the easiest ways to add texture, colour, and pattern, table linens can transform the look and mood of a meal. If you have trouble choosing, you can never go wrong with softer colours and timeless patterns that you won't tire of too quickly.

Table linens should be washable, and cotton tends to be the easiest to care for. Linen is lovely, but it wrinkles easily and requires extra ironing if you want to keep it crisp. Damask is one of the most formal and traditional choices. Made with silk, linen, and other natural fibres, it has a reversible pattern woven into it.

For a perfectly pressed tablecloth, dampen the fabric with warm water, lay it over a fluffy towel, and press with a steam iron.

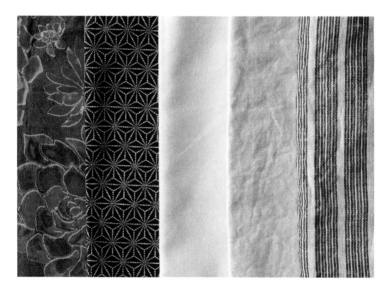

TABLECLOTHS

As a general rule, these should drop 30–40 centimetres from the edge of the table.

NAPKINS

These can be folded, rolled, tucked into glasses, or held together with rings. The presentation possibilities are endless.

Common Sizes

DINNER
56–66 centimetres square

LUNCHEON
35–45 centimetres square

COCKTAIL
10–15 centimetres square

RUNNERS

One of the most flexible options, they fit on any size table or sideboard.

PLACE MATS

More casual than a tablecloth, these protect the surface of the table and visually divide it into place settings.

A NOTE ON MONOGRAMS

A single letter (traditionally the first letter of the last name) is simple and elegant. The most common placement is either on the lower right-hand corner or directly in the centre of the napkins.

PUTTING IT ALL
TOGETHER

The Casual Setting

An informal setting has only a few pieces, and everything that's needed throughout the meal should be laid out at once. It's good for family-style spreads and dinners that don't require re-setting during the meal. As a general rule for any occasion (casual or formal), plates and cutlery should be placed about 1 centimetre apart, with the bottoms lined up about 2 centimetres from the edge of the table. Each person should be given about 60 centimetres of table space to avoid feeling crowded.

1 | **DINNER PLATE**

2 | **NAPKIN**

3 | **DINNER FORK**

4 | **DINNER KNIFE**

5 | **DESSERT SPOON**

6 | **WATER GLASS**

7 | **WINE GLASS**

Napkin rings are a quick way to keep linens neat and pulled together.

The Formal Setting

A formal table setting requires a more hands-on approach when it comes to serving. Often, there are many pieces on the table to begin with, and plates and cutlery need to be cleared between courses. Settings for no more than three courses should be laid out at a time. Forks, knives, and spoons are always placed in order of use, from the outside in.

1 | **DINNER PLATE**

2 | **SALAD PLATE**

3 | **BREAD-AND-BUTTER PLATE**

4 | **BREAD KNIFE**

5 | **SALAD FORK**

6 | **DINNER FORK**

7 | **DINNER KNIFE**

8 | **SOUP SPOON**

9 | **DESSERT SPOON**

10 | **WHITE WINE GLASS**

11 | **WATER GLASS**

12 | **RED WINE GLASS**

13 | **NAPKIN**

14 | **PLACE CARD**

Plates are served to the left of guests and cleared from the right. All plates, serving dishes, and condiments should be removed from the table before the pudding course is served.

Mixing & Matching

This is where table setting gets playful. Generally, white dinner plates are the most versatile and put the spotlight on the food. Plates for serving the pudding course are a good place to experiment with pattern, as a slice of chocolate cake will look good on just about anything. White or neutral serving pieces lighten up the table. Colourful ones make more of a statement.

USING COLOUR

When picking palettes, consider the colours in the room where you eat. Complementary colours (the ones on opposite sides of the colour wheel) always work well together. And don't forget to think about scale by balancing complex designs and saturated solids with something more neutral.

If you're buying a tea or luncheon plate set, choose different patterns so you have more options (they're almost the same size and can be used interchangeably).

COLLECTING ANTIQUES

Treasures can be found at house clearances, charity shops, and in your gran's attic. Look out for serving pieces, silverware, cut or coloured glass, and pretty plates and platters. Before you buy, always check antique pieces carefully (both top and bottom) for chips, hairlines, and cracks.

If you stick with a cohesive palette, it's easier to mix patterns. Pick solid plates that pick up on a colour in something printed.

INCORPORATING HEIRLOOMS

For an eclectic look, mix antique silver pieces together. Or pair vintage plates for the pudding course with newer dinnerware.

TONAL TEXTURE

All-white doesn't have to be boring.
Patterns in relief and simple borders
add depth and dimension.

Folding Napkins

There are endless ways to present napkins at the table, from intricate designs to casual folds. We've included a couple of our favourites here.

It's considered polite to place your napkin on your chair if you need to get up during a meal.

THE DIAMOND FOLD

1 | Lay the napkin face down in front of you. Fold it in half from top to bottom, and then again from left to right. You should have a smaller square with the open end facing towards you.

2 | Fold back the top layer so that its bottom right corner touches the upper left-hand corner of the napkin.

3 | Fold back the second layer just as you did the first, but stop slightly short of the last fold to create an even but staggered effect. Repeat until you have folded back all of the remaining layers.

4 | Rotate the napkin clockwise until the point of the triangle shape is at the top. Flip the napkin over. Fold both bottom corners towards the top centre point, overlapping them a little so you end up with a five-sided diamond shape. Carefully turn the napkin over and flatten or iron it. Place the napkin on the plate.

If you have herbs left over from cooking, you can use them to decorate the table.

THE SINGLE POCKET FOLD

1 | Lay the napkin face down in front of you. Fold the napkin in half from the bottom to the top to form a rectangle with the open end facing away from you.

2 | Fold the top layer halfway back. Flip the napkin over.

3 | Fold the napkin in half from the right to the left, and then in half again from right to left.

4 | Carefully flip the napkin over. Tie a piece of twine into a bow round the bottom half of the napkin. Insert a fresh sprig of rosemary or another herb or flower as an embellishment. Slide a menu card under the herb and place the napkin on the plate.

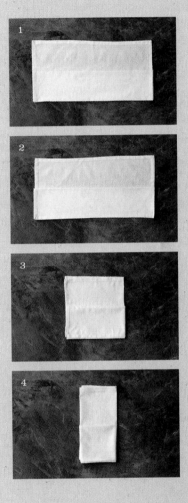

Finishing Touches

Whatever decorations you choose,
remember that they shouldn't distract
from the food or conversation.

CANDLES
Tea lights in a variety of glass holders create a magical
effect, while a pair of cream-coloured dinner candles
placed in candlesticks add a touch of elegance.

*A tip for selecting
flowers: choose
something that's
in season and
complements a colour
from your dishes
or linens.*

FLOWERS & GARLANDS

Keep arrangements low enough that they
don't block guests from talking across the
table. If you have a large centrepiece, remove
it just before the guests take their seats.

NATURAL INGREDIENTS

Anything pretty and fresh that's used to
make a meal can also be used to decorate
a place setting.

The
DINING TABLE

SUNDAY
LUNCH

It's a pleasure to end the week
with a large, casual meal for
family and friends. Set a simple
table with large plates, basic
linens, and serving dishes so
guests can help themselves.

---

*Cold, leftover roasted meats are perfect
for weekday lunches, either as sandwich
fillings, served with salads, or used as
pie fillings. Set out containers before
dinner, so they're easy to fill when
everyone has finished.*

Table **TALK**

THE TRADITION OF ROASTING A JOINT FOR SUNDAY LUNCH ORIGINATED IN BRITAIN BECAUSE MANY ANGLICANS AND ROMAN CATHOLICS ABSTAINED FROM EATING MEAT FROM FRIDAY NIGHT UNTIL AFTER CHURCH ON SUNDAY. SUNDAY LUNCH WAS A CELEBRATORY MEAL EATEN AFTER THE SERVICE WHEN THE FAST WAS FINALLY BROKEN.

THE FOUNDATION
OF A FAMILY-STYLE FEAST

PLATTERS FOR SERVING
A roasting dish that can go straight from the oven
to the table means less washing up later.

BOWLS TO PASS
Place serving utensils in the serving bowls so it's easy for
guests to help themselves, and always pass to the right.

SMALL DISHES FOR BUTTER,
SALT, AND PEPPER
Salt and pepper should travel as a pair. Make sure
to taste the food before adding extra seasoning.

SEATED
DINNER
PARTY

For special occasions, or just because, a meal served in courses doesn't need to be complicated. A palette of white and gold is a clean and classic look and allows the food to take centre stage.

Traditionally, the dinner plate is brought out after the first course and charger are cleared. However, for something simpler, layer the dinner plate with a tea or luncheon plate, which can be removed after the starter.

THE BASICS FOR A FORMAL (NOT FUSSY) AFFAIR

PLACE CARDS

Use these for parties of eight or more. A menu card is
a nice way to guide guests through multiple courses.

---

*The host or hostess generally sits at the head of the table
where he or she can see and engage with all of the guests.*

GLASSES

Set the water glass to the right of the plate just above the
knife. Wine glasses are set to the right of the water glass, in
the order that they will be used.

CUTLERY

Once used, silver shouldn't touch the table.
Rest it on the edge of a plate or saucer instead.

FOLDED NAPKINS

Place on your lap as soon as you are seated.

Table **TALK** ALWAYS WAIT UNTIL EVERYONE HAS BEEN SERVED
BEFORE YOU START EATING, AND DON'T CLEAR
PLATES BEFORE THE LAST GUEST HAS FINISHED.

BANK
HOLIDAY
BREAKFAST

On long weekends, you might
want to serve a more elaborate
morning meal. Start with plates, a
small bowl, and a napkin at each
place, and set the table with fresh
flowers that celebrate the season.

---

*For make-your-own brunch cocktails,
arrange a simple bar on a side table with
juices, Bloody Mary mixture, vodka, and
champagne for making Buck's Fizz.*

ESSENTIALS FOR
CHRISTMAS MORNING

FRENCH PRESS CAFETIERE
Keep things easy and use the same piece for
brewing and serving at the table.

MULTIPURPOSE TUMBLERS
A simple glass works for water, juice,
Buck's Fizz, or milk.

SERVING DISHES
Prepare food on cutting boards and in ovenware that
can go straight from the kitchen to the table.

CLEAR BOTTLES & GLASSES
Decant condiments such as cranberry sauce
for a tidier look.

The
BREAKFAST BAR

APPETIZERS & COCKTAILS

If you don't have a lot of space, spread out antipasto and other small bites on a breakfast bar or butcher's block. Stack salad or bread-and-butter plates so people can help themselves.

A mixture of mismatched plates makes it easy for guests to remember whose is whose if they rest them on a side or coffee table.

THE ELEMENTS OF
A SIMPLE COCKTAIL BAR

TRAY AS A BAR

A bar trolley isn't necessary as you can just use a tray to
hold liquor, shakers, and stir sticks.

----

*A few classic mixers to always have on hand:
lime cordial, ginger beer, tonic water (in small bottles,
so it doesn't go flat), soda water, bitters.*

A MIXTURE OF COCKTAIL GLASSES

Don't worry if you don't have complete sets. Simply
put out a selection and let guests choose the
style they like best.

MISMATCHED SILVER & TONGS

Use a mixture of vintage and new silver for canapés.

WEEKEND BREAKFAST

Especially good when you have company, a help-yourself spread is ready whether guests get up early or have a lie-in.

Lay out stacks of plates, bowls, and mugs the night before, along with cereal, sugar, and jams.

Keep a basket with milk, yoghurt, and butter in the fridge, and leave a note explaining where to find things.

WAYS TO MAKE OVERNIGHT GUESTS FEEL AT HOME

COFFEE MAKER & MUGS

Set up the coffee maker the night before so guests can switch it on and help themselves the next morning.

EGG CUPS FOR SERVING

Hard-boil eggs the night before and leave them out in pretty cups.

A CONTAINER FOR CUTLERY

Use a mason jar, wide-mouthed glass, or mug to keep knives, forks, and spoons neatly together.

Table **TALK** — MAKE SURE A COVERED JAR OF FRESHLY GROUND BEANS IS NEARBY.

MIDNIGHT
BITES

Late at night is the perfect time for leftovers and a cold drink – the adult version of a bedtime snack. Instead of standing over the sink or eating directly from the takeaway container, serve everything from the breakfast bar. Put the pizza onto plates, pour the beer into glasses, and use real linens.

Fresh tea towels from the kitchen make great stand-ins for place mats and napkins.

NIGHTTIME SNACK SUPPLIES

PINCH BOWLS FOR SEASONING
Fill with salt, Parmesan, or chilli flakes.

GLASSES FOR WINE OR BEER
Pour bottled beer into tumblers or stemmed goblets.

SMALL PLATES
Use anything except paper – even fine china.

Soak dishes in the sink before going to bed to make washing up easier in the morning.

The
COFFEE TABLE

TUESDAY
TAKEAWAY

Easy-to-eat noodle and rice
dishes are perfect for perching
on a coffee table. It's a nice
touch to plate up the food and
decant sauces before serving.

---

*Coasters are an easy way to add pattern.
Use them under glasses and small dishes
of sauces.*

THE DETAILS IN
DECANTING DELIVERY

A RUNNER FOR SMALLER TABLES
Long and narrow, it fits on almost any surface.
As an alternative, use tea towels or unfolded
napkins as place mats.

DINNERWARE AS SERVING DISHES
Dinner plates and cereal bowls are just the right
size for smaller portions.

CHOPSTICKS
Rest them on the edge of your plate when
you're not using them.

Table **TALK** — HOLD THE UPPER CHOPSTICK LIKE A PENCIL, BETWEEN YOUR THUMB AND INDEX FINGER, JUST ABOVE THE MIDDLE. THE SECOND CHOPSTICK SHOULD BE PARALLEL, HELD AGAINST YOUR RING FINGER AND THE BASE OF YOUR THUMB.

FILM NIGHT

Elevate a night of Netflix or celebrate the Oscars with snacks served in porcelain in an Art Deco style, and offer drinks in fancy glasses.

Place tea lights in antique-effect glass holders for a warm shiny glow.

AN OSCAR NIGHT
ARRANGEMENT

NAPKINS & RINGS

Think of napkin rings as jewellery for the table.
Play with different shapes and materials as you
would a stack of bangles or dress rings.

A SOUP TUREEN FOR POPCORN

Repurpose a vintage piece for serving snacks.

A MIXTURE OF PATTERNED PLATES & BOWLS

Flaunt your best porcelain – even if it doesn't match.

---

*Decorative dessert plates can be expensive and might
seem extravagant to purchase as a set. Instead, just buy
a few and use them as accents.*

WINE &
CHEESE

Served before dinner, after dinner, or as a meal on its own, wine and cheese is the perfect spread for a coffee table, where food can be nibbled and nothing needs to be cut.

To build a cheese board, choose at least three varieties. Include a mixture of hard and soft cheeses, along with a separate knife for each.

THE PERFECT ASSORTMENT

CHEESE BOARD
Slate is a nice alternative to wood, and you can
use chalk to write the names of the cheese.

A BOWL USED AS AN ICE BUCKET
Almost any large serving bowl will work for this. Choose
something patterned for a pop of colour.

---

*Chill white wine ahead of time and open a few bottles before guests
arrive. Some white wines aren't meant to be ice cold, so ask your
wine merchant or check the label for the ideal temperature.*

A MIXTURE OF GLASSES
Mix stemmed styles with tumblers for a casual
vibe (or if you don't have a complete set).

SMALL BOWLS AND SPOONS
Use these for serving nuts, olives, chutney, and biscuits for
cheese. Don't forget one for olive pits.

The

PICNIC BLANKET

BIRTHDAY PICNIC

Gather things together in a
basket, including a fancy cake
stand and champagne coupes.
Then make your way to the
park or out into your garden.

*Make transporting everything easier
by asking each guest to contribute. Have
someone bring the cake and candles,
ask someone else to take care of the
champagne and glasses, and so on.*

FESTIVE TOUCHES

PICNIC BASKET

Fill it with china and glasses instead of paper picnicware.
Wrap fabric napkins around the champagne coupes to pad
them while carrying them to the park.

Table
TALK

THE CHAMPAGNE COUPE HAS A VINTAGE VIBE. IT WAS
INTRODUCED IN FRANCE DURING THE EIGHTEENTH
CENTURY AND BY THE 1930S HAD FOUND WIDESPREAD
POPULARITY AMONG CHAMPAGNE DRINKERS

LINENS & BLANKETS

Use real tablecloths and napkins but be sure to layer them
over a heavier picnic blanket to avoid grass stains.

CAKE STAND

Top with a birthday cake, or put candles into stacks of
cupcakes or muffins, to make them feel festive.

SUMMER BBQ

Cooking outdoors should feel relaxed. Keep the menu simple and allow guests to help themselves to the food.

A good playlist – nothing too loud or too slow – keeps the momentum going throughout the meal without distracting from conversation. Think about how long the party will last and make sure there are enough songs to fill the time.

OUTDOOR DINING BASICS

PLATES

Repurpose extra dinner plates as trays for toppings
and side dishes. Use smaller sizes for spoon rests.

JAM JARS FOR CONDIMENTS

Fill covered containers to transport ketchup, mustard,
and chutneys in just the right portions.

WOODEN TRAYS FOR BREAD

Something long and narrow is great for laying
out hamburger buns.

BBQ TOOLS

Use the same utensils (tongs, spatulas, and spoons)
to cook and to serve.

The

BISTRO TABLE

WEEKDAY BREAKFAST

Even on a busy morning when there's no time to cook, it can be such a pleasure to sit down to breakfast. A plate, spoon, and coffee cup are all you really need, but adding egg cups, juice glasses, and linens add a touch of luxury.

Set out dishes the night before so everything's ready to go when you get up.

THE MORNING MIX

BOWLS

One of the most versatile dishes, they can be used to serve almost anything.

For a Parisian twist, drink coffee out of small bowls instead of mugs.

TABLE LINENS

A runner fits on any table, regardless of size.

To keep cloth napkins, runners, and place mats smooth, store them wrapped round a cardboard tube.

CUPS FOR EGGS

If you don't have traditional egg cups, espresso cups are a similar size and will work just as well.

DINNER
FOR TWO

Don't save the fine china just for special occasions. Use it for dinner any day of the week. A simple two-course meal feels intimate served on a small bistro table. It can be charming to mix up sets of plates and play with different patterns.

Make it feel like a local restaurant: use a white tablecloth, light a single candle, and fill a small bud vase with fresh flowers.

DATE-NIGHT INSPIRATION

TEA LIGHT HOLDERS FOR CANDLES AND FLOWERS

An easy way to set the mood and create the most flattering light.

PRETTY PLATES

Layer different styles – interesting edges stand out against a pattern and colour.

A BASKET OR BOWL FOR BREAD

Line it with a linen napkin to keep rolls covered and warm.

A PLATE FOR BUTTER

Pick a small saucer or tea or luncheon plate if you don't have a designated dish.

Table **TALK**

USE A BUTTER KNIFE TO PUT A PORTION ONTO YOUR PLATE – NEVER SPREAD BUTTER DIRECTLY ONTO THE BREAD.

The

CONSOLE

DESSERT &
CHAMPAGNE

A sideboard or a console table
will work as a serving station for
after-dinner treats. Set out
platters of cakes, biscuits, and
other baked goods with stacks
of small plates and napkins.

---

*For an easy cocktail that guests can
make themselves, provide a simple herbal
or fruit syrup to mix with champagne.
Also include sparkling mineral water as
a non-alcoholic option.*

IDEAS FOR A SPARKLING CELEBRATION

TIERED STANDS

If you have any special serving pieces, use them
to add height – a decorative stand makes
even the simplest cake look fancy.

ICE BUCKET

Keep this at the edge of the table so guests can easily refill
their glasses themselves.

---

*To chill champagne quickly, put the bottle in a mixture
of water and ice.*

TRAYS AND BOARDS

Mix materials – marble, brass, wood, or lacquer –
to add texture and colour.

OPEN HOUSE

If hosting a dinner party with lots of guests seems daunting, an open house is an easy way to entertain. Hours are usually open-ended, so you don't need to rush to get everything on the table at a certain time. People will come and go, creating a casual, laid-back vibe.

Open houses are common around the holidays, but you can hold one any time. Plan something around a graduation, a housewarming, or a big game.

TIPS FOR EASY
ENTERTAINING

SERVING BOWLS
Set each dish out next to any seasoning or
condiments that might be needed. Place a cutting
board nearby for resting serving spoons.

———————————

*Texture and height are important on buffets. Fruit punnets from
farmer's markets make great risers, napkin holders, or bread baskets.*

A PUNCH BOWL
Mix drinks ahead of time and invite guests
to serve themselves using a ladle.

CUTLERY
Bundle sets up in napkins and tie with simple
twine so they're easy to pick up.

POTLUCK DINNER

Serve dinner from a buffet if you don't have a big table, and ask guests to bring a dish. It's important to lay things out in the order that people will serve themselves, with plates at the beginning and utensils at the end.

Party ideas: pick a theme or cuisine for the night. Or start a cooking club to exchange recipes and where everyone takes it in turn to act as host.

CROWD-PLEASING PIECES

SERVING BOWLS & PLATTERS

Keep dressings next to salads and seasonings
near main courses.

---

*If possible, leave some space between each
dish so people can put down their plate and use
both hands for serving.*

CHARGERS AS DINNER PLATES

The larger size lends itself to bigger portions.

CUTLERY ROLLED IN NAPKINS

These should be stacked at the end of the buffet for guests
to collect after they've filled their plate.

The

SERVING TRAY

BREAKFAST
IN BED

This is a sweet surprise for special days. Pick a tray that's just large enough to hold everything comfortably and is easy to carry from the kitchen to the bedroom.

Keep the menu simple. Focus on things you can prepare ahead of time, hot foods that cook quickly, like scrambled eggs, ready-made pastries such as croissants, and things that are good at room temperature, such as fruit, yoghurt, and muesli.

LAZY MORNING MUST-HAVES

STURDY DISHES
Choose bowls and mugs with wide bottoms for stability,
and plates that are large enough to catch crumbs.

A CARAFE OR SMALL JUG FOR REFILLS
Include extra coffee, juice, or water so you don't
need to run back to the kitchen for a top-up.

———

*Avoid using stemmed glasses or anything top heavy
that might tip over.*

A GLASS FOR FLOWERS
Keep decorations minimal. A single flower or petite
bouquet in a bottle, water glass, or bud vase
is perfect for small spaces.

AFTERNOON TEA

Traditionally served around three or four, afternoon tea is a child-friendly occasion that precedes cocktail hour. Use a tray to transport a teapot, cups, milk, and sugar to the sitting room, conservatory, or even the garden, on a sunny afternoon.

Table **TALK**

AFTERNOON TEA BECAME POPULAR IN THE NINETEENTH CENTURY. AS LEGEND GOES, IT STARTED WHEN ANNA MARIA RUSSELL, DUCHESS OF BEDFORD, NEEDED A PICK-ME-UP BETWEEN LUNCH AND A LATE DINNER. HER FRIENDS STARTED JOINING HER AND EVENTUALLY IT BECAME A SOCIAL AFFAIR.

TEATIME NECESSITIES

TEAPOT

It doesn't need to be from the same collection
as the cups and saucers. Mix in vintage pieces
or family heirlooms.

———————————

*Include a jug or pot of hot water for those
who like to dilute their tea.*

TEACUPS & SAUCERS

Make sure each guest has his or her own teaspoon
for stirring in milk and sugar.

SERVING PLATES

Stack them and layer each with a cocktail
napkin to save space.

A SUGAR BOWL, MILK JUG & SAUCER
FOR LEMON SLICES

Pair loose sugar with a spoon, sugar cubes with tongs,
and citrus slices with a small fork.

Resources

AMAZON
amazon.com
amazon.co.uk

ANTHROPOLOGIE*
anthropologie.com

APARTMENT THERAPY FOR CANVAS*
apartmenttherapy.com

BED BATH & BEYOND
bedbathandbeyond.com

BERNARDAUD
bernardaud.com

BLOOMINGDALE'S
bloomingdales.com

CHILEWICH (PLACE MAT)*
chilewich.com

CLAM LAB (CERAMICS)*
clamlab.com

COX AND COX
coxandcox.co.uk

CRATE & BARREL
crateandbarrel.com

CUTIPOL CUTLERY*
cutipol.pt

DUNELM
dunelm.com

HABITAT
habitat.co.uk

JOHN LEWIS
johnlewis.com

JOY
joythestore.com

KATE SPADE*
katespade.com

LAKELAND
lakeland.co.uk

LENOX*
lenox.com

MACY'S*
macys.com

OLIVER BONAS
oliverbonas.com

POTTERY BARN
potterybarn.com

SELFRIDGES
selfridges.com

TARGET*
target.com

URBAN OUTFITTERS*
urbanoutfitters.com

WILLIAMS SONOMA*
williams-sonoma.com

WEST ELM*
westelm.com

A SPECIAL THANK-YOU TO THESE ADVISORS AND CONSULTANTS:

Kristen Usui (kristenusui.com), for her gorgeous flower arrangements, and Shadow at J-Rose Wholesale Flowers, for donating the flowers

Kristin Perrakis, Jean Armstrong, and Michael Schwarz, for lending props from Williams Sonoma

Naomi Nomikos at Bardith

Sophie Raubiet at Bernardaud

Nathalie Smith at Global Table

Jamie Erickson at Poppy's

1 3 5 7 9 10 8 6 4 2

Ebury Press, an imprint of Ebury Publishing,
20 Vauxhall Bridge Road, London SW1V 2SA

Ebury Press is part of the Penguin Random House group
of companies whose addresses can be found at global.
penguinrandomhouse.com

Penguin
Random House
UK

Written by Chloe Lieske
Interior photographs by Alpha Smoot
Illustrations by woolypear
Prop styling by Maeve Sheridan
Floral styling by Kristen Usui
Cover and interior design by Danielle Deschenes

First published by Clarkson Potter in 2017
This edition published by Ebury Press in 2017

www.penguin.co.uk

A CIP catalogue record for this book is available from the
British Library

ISBN 978 1 785 03748 1

Printed and bound in China by Toppan Leefung